PREH... ...RI
FLYING ...TERS

Liz Miles

W
FRANKLIN WATTS
LONDON•SYDNEY

First published in paperback in 2013

First published in 2012 by Franklin Watts
Copyright © 2012 Arcturus Publishing Limited

Franklin Watts
338 Euston Road
London NW1 3BH
Franklin Watts Australia
Level 17/207 Kent Street, Sydney NSW 2000

Produced by Arcturus Publishing Limited,
26/27 Bickels Yard, 151–153 Bermondsey Street, London SE1 3HA

Text: Liz Miles
Editor: Joe Harris
Picture researcher: Joe Harris
Design: Emma Randall
Cover design: Emma Randall

Picture credits:
Corbis: 2–3, 10–11, 13br, 29 row 6 r. pixel-shack.com: cover (main), 1, 5tr, 6–7, 7cr, 8–9, 12–13, 14–15, 16–17, 18–19, 20–21, 24–25, 26–27, 28t, 29 row 2l, 29 row 2r, 29 row 3l, 29 row 3r, 29 row 4l, 29 row 5l, 29 row 6r. Science Photo Library: 15tr, 15br, 17br, 19tr, 22–23. Shutterstock: cover (all top), 4–5, 5cr, 5br, 7tr, 11cr, 11br, 17tr, 25tr, 29 row 1. Wikimedia: 7br, 9tr, 9cr, 9br, 11tr, 13tr, 13cr, 17cr, 19br, 21tr, 21br, 23tr, 23br, 25br, 27tr, 27br, 29 row 4 r.

A CIP catalogue record for this book is available from the British Library.

Dewey Decimal Classification Number 567.9'18-dc23

ISBN 978 1 4451 2348 6

Printed in China

Franklin Watts is a division of Hachette Children's Books, an Hachette UK company.

www.hachette.co.uk

SL001832EN
Supplier 03, Date 0213, Print Run 2399

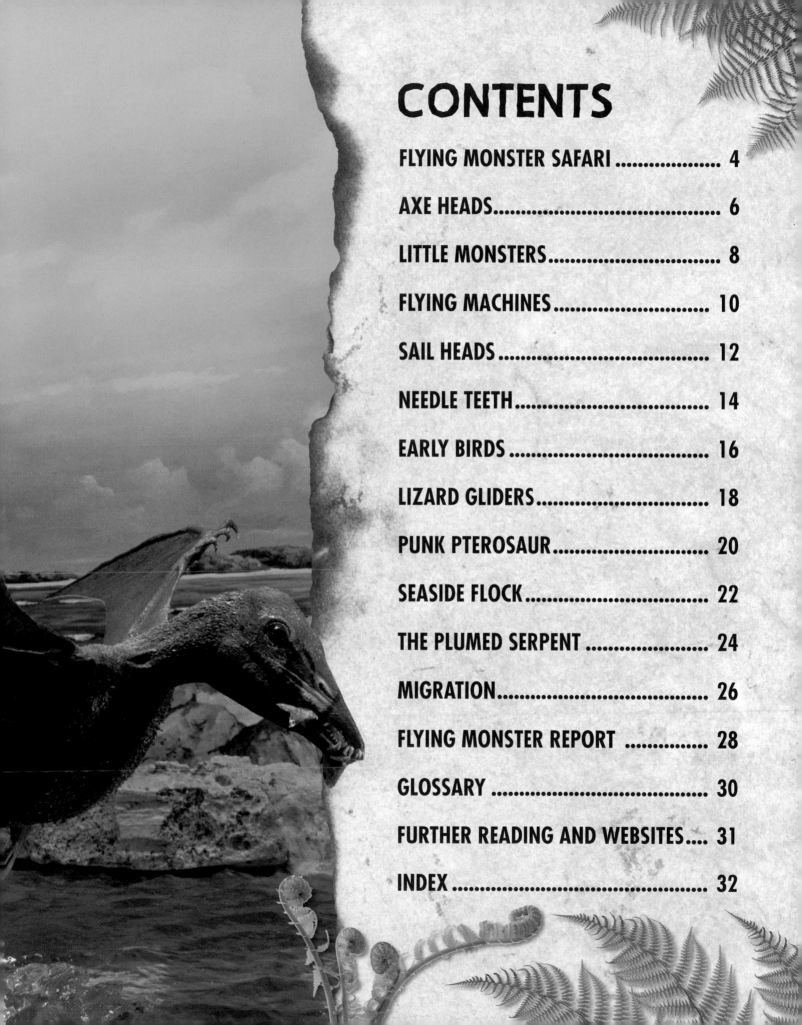

CONTENTS

FLYING MONSTER SAFARI

Get ready for an aerial thrill ride! You're about to face the most dangerous challenge of your life – exploring a remote island, rumoured to be the home of flying reptiles. Until now, these reptiles were thought to have disappeared 65 million years ago. Your mission is to film these terrifying creatures.

You're going to need wings of your own to get as close as you dare to the pterosaurs ('winged lizards'). So you take to the air in a microlight — a small, open plane.

You will be flying alongside giants that have wingspans the size of fighter jets, and snapping jaws that could swallow you whole.

SAFARI ESSENTIALS

Protective clothing A pilot helmet for flight is essential. You also have claw-proof clothing for when you track pterosaurs at ground level.

Video camera You can fix this camera to the cockpit of the microlight to record the flying creatures in mid-air.

dinoPad Your special e-book reader holds all information known about prehistoric animals, including these awesome flying creatures.

AXE HEADS

You approach the island at a steady speed. Suddenly, you aren't alone: three pterosaurs like beaked dragons surround the microlight and seem to guide you into their ominous world. You recognise the *Pteranodons'* pickaxe-shaped heads. Each waft of their giant wings nearly sends your craft off course, so you take a dive to escape.

Pteranodon's huge wings are made up of leathery membranes supported by muscles and bones.

Monster-size *Pteranodon* have a wingspan of up to 9 m (30 ft) — that's as wide as your microlight.

Some *Pteranodon* have long crests. Perhaps they act as rudders in flight, or balance the weight of their long jaws.

The *Pteranodon*'s head is longer than its body, with long, toothless jaws for catching fish.

Pteranodon has featured in many movies, including *Jurassic Park III.*

Meaning of name: Toothless wing
Size: 9 m (30 ft) wingspan
Family: Pteranodontidae
Period: Late Cretaceous
Weight: 9–14 kg (20–30 lb)
Found in: North America
Diet: Fish

FACT AND FICTION

▼ **Snapping beaks** Unlike those shown in many movies, real *Pteranodon* have no teeth. However, if a *Pteranodon* mistook you for a fish, it could eat most of you in one gulp with its 1.2 m- (4 ft-) long jaws.

► **Grabbing claws** Movies that show human beings being carried away in the claws of *Pteranodon* are not based on evidence. The *Pteranodon*'s rear claws are not strong enough to carry a human!

◄ **Crest shapes** *Pteranodon* are nearly always shown with long crests on their heads. However, the sizes and shapes of fossilised crests vary greatly.

LITTLE MONSTERS

As you dive and the *Pteranodon* leave, you hit a cloud of buzzing, biting insects. Worse still, the insects are prey to a flock of seagull-sized *Anurognathus,* which soon flap around your head, obscuring the view through your visor. Your helmet protects your head but an *Anurognathus* nips your neck. While hardly able to see, you must attempt a landing...

Anurognathus has very strong jaws for feeding on insects while in flight.

Meaning of name: Frog jaw
Size: 50 cm (20 in) wingspan
Family: Anurognathidea
Period: Late Jurassic
Weight: 80–160 g (3–6 oz)
Found in: Europe
Diet: Insects

Anurognathus' tail is short so that it doesn't get in the way while the creature hunts for insects like beetles and flies.

TINY TERRORS

▼ ***Anurognathus*** is in the first group of pterosaurs to evolve, the rhamphorhynchoids. These creatures are often small. Some of them feed on the insects buzzing around dinosaurs' heads.

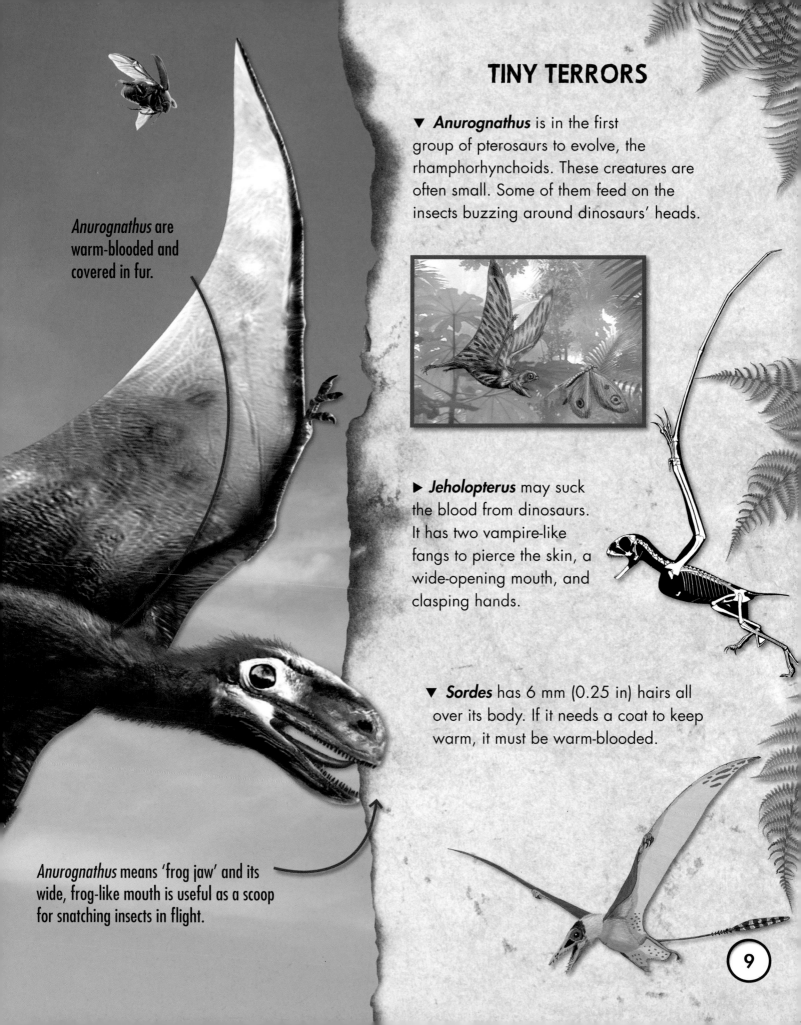

Anurognathus are warm-blooded and covered in fur.

▶ ***Jeholopterus*** may suck the blood from dinosaurs. It has two vampire-like fangs to pierce the skin, a wide-opening mouth, and clasping hands.

▼ ***Sordes*** has 6 mm (0.25 in) hairs all over its body. If it needs a coat to keep warm, it must be warm-blooded.

Anurognathus means 'frog jaw' and its wide, frog-like mouth is useful as a scoop for snatching insects in flight.

FLYING MACHINES

You land on bumpy ground, and taxi to a halt near a riverside. You grab your camera as you leave the plane, ready to film an incredible gathering. A flock of *Eudimorphodon* is snapping up fish. You gasp at their amazing flying skills, but on the ground they are clumsy and can hardly walk. Suddenly they all panic – there are splashes and squawks. What has startled them?

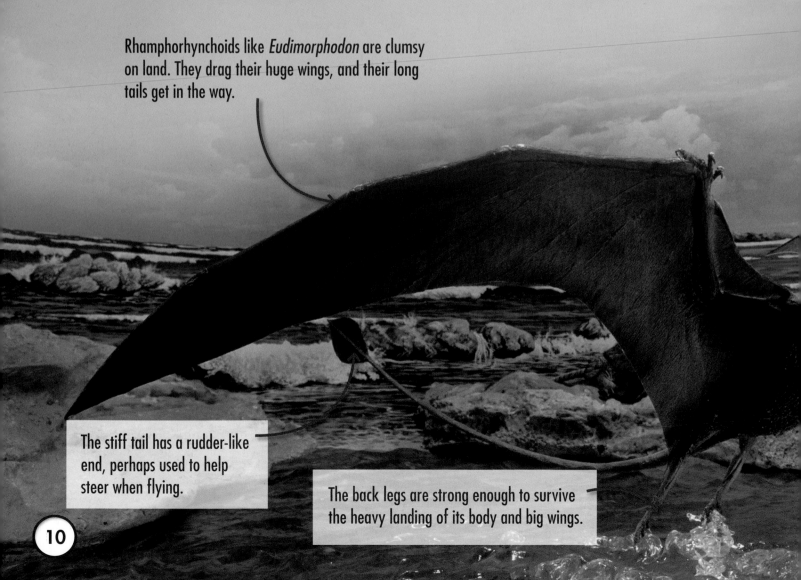

Rhamphorhynchoids like *Eudimorphodon* are clumsy on land. They drag their huge wings, and their long tails get in the way.

The stiff tail has a rudder-like end, perhaps used to help steer when flying.

The back legs are strong enough to survive the heavy landing of its body and big wings.

Eudimorphodon is one of the earliest living pterosaurs known.

Meaning of name: True two-formed tooth
Size: 1 m (3 ft) wingspan
Family: Campylognathoididae
Period: Late Triassic
Weight: 1 kg (2 lb)
Found in: Europe
Diet: Fish

There are more than a hundred teeth in the mouth of a *Eudimorphodon*. There are fangs near the front — perfect for grabbing slippery fish.

MASTERS OF THE SKY

The earliest pterosaurs were gliders. *Eudimorphodon* was among the first to master true flight.

▶ Some pterosaurs use their feet to hang from trees and to take off from branches or cliff faces.

▶ Although pterosaurs are bat-like in many ways, they have more control over their wings than bats, and are more stable fliers.

◀ Many pterosaurs prey on fish. They are able to dive down and take a bite from the sea without free-falling.

SAIL HEADS

The flock of *Eudimorphodon* scatter at the sight of this majestic monster – a *Nyctosaurus*. The sail on its head is as big as a yacht's. As you film it nervously, you wonder why it has such a huge crest. Perhaps it's just there to impress – it certainly scared off the competition. Now it has the river fish to itself.

With a wingspan of up to 3 m (10 ft), *Nyctosaurus* cruises low over the water at a speed of about 35 kph (20 mph).

The antler-like bone struts in the sail are up to three times the length of the skull.

Unlike most pterosaurs, *Nyctosaurus* does not have claws that can grasp, so it can't land on a tree or cling to a cliff.

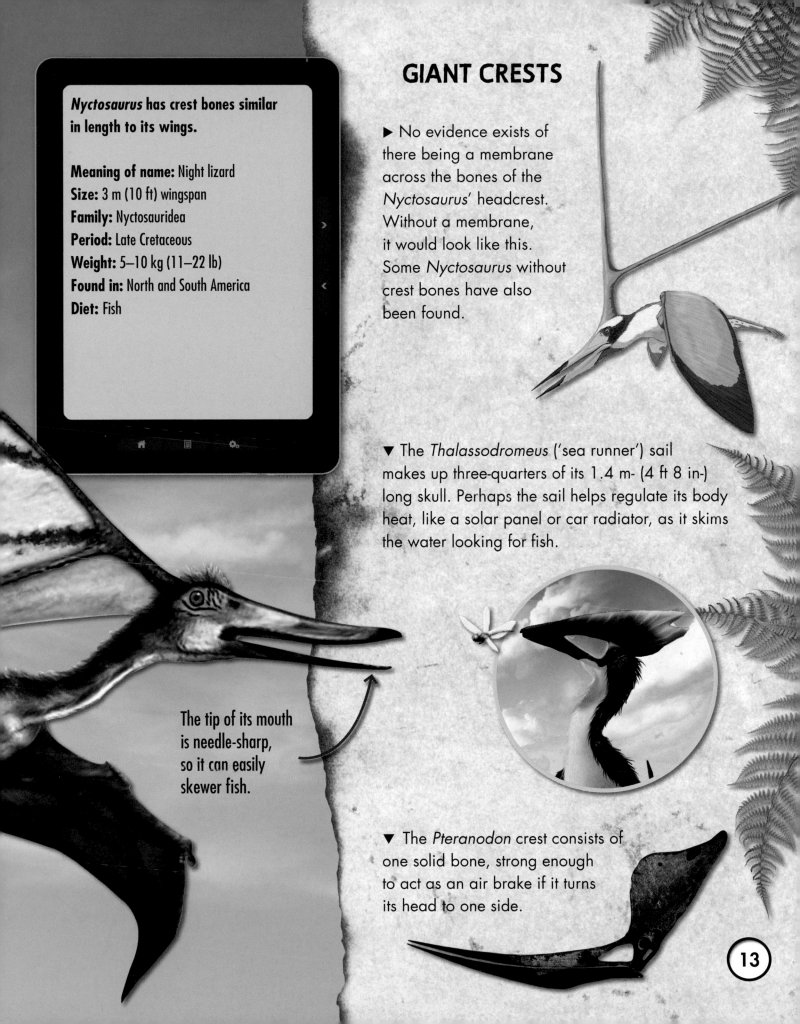

Nyctosaurus has crest bones similar in length to its wings.

Meaning of name: Night lizard
Size: 3 m (10 ft) wingspan
Family: Nyctosauridea
Period: Late Cretaceous
Weight: 5–10 kg (11–22 lb)
Found in: North and South America
Diet: Fish

GIANT CRESTS

▶ No evidence exists of there being a membrane across the bones of the *Nyctosaurus'* headcrest. Without a membrane, it would look like this. Some *Nyctosaurus* without crest bones have also been found.

▼ The *Thalassodromeus* ('sea runner') sail makes up three-quarters of its 1.4 m- (4 ft 8 in-) long skull. Perhaps the sail helps regulate its body heat, like a solar panel or car radiator, as it skims the water looking for fish.

The tip of its mouth is needle-sharp, so it can easily skewer fish.

▼ The *Pteranodon* crest consists of one solid bone, strong enough to act as an air brake if it turns its head to one side.

NEEDLE TEETH

There's an ear-splitting squawk – you spin round to see a pterosaur nearly twice as big as the *Nyctosaurus*. It's a *Cearadactylus*! You lie flat as it dives towards the river. Your hands are shaking, but you keep the camera running. There's just time to capture those needle-sharp teeth and crocodile-like jaws. Then it swoops straight at you! You run for shelter.

Cearadactylus' wingspan is at least three times your height.

Cearadactylus has long jaws like a crocodile's, which suggests it ate fish.

Meaning of name: Ceará finger (Ceará is a Brazilian state.)
Size: 6 m (20 ft) wingspan
Family: Ornithocheiridae
Period: Middle Cretaceous
Weight: 14–18 kg (30–40 lb)
Found in: South America
Diet: Fish

Like many pterosaurs, *Cearadactylus* lays eggs.

CRUSHERS AND SCOOPERS

Even the largest pterosaurs are little heavier than the largest birds alive today. They have hollow bones only about 1 mm (0.04 in) thick.

▼ *Dsungaripterus* has a narrow, upward-pointing beak for opening shellfish, and bony knobs instead of teeth act as shell and bone crushers.

▼ *Pterodaustro* is like a flamingo, scooping and filtering its food using a large beak. The lower jaw has brush-like bristles that work like a sieve.

Cearadactylus' jaws have small interlocking teeth, with a cage of longer teeth at the front to stop fish slipping away.

EARLY BIRDS

You keep running until you reach the safety of a forest. There's a rustle amongst the trees – you jump, then laugh, as a strange turkey-like creature flutters down from a branch and lands heavily at your feet. It looks at you before flapping off. You can hardly believe it. You've just seen one of the first birds – the *Archaeopteryx*! You follow it, leaving your microlight further behind …

Weak flight muscles mean it cannot fly as well as a pterosaur. It flutters short distances, walks on the ground and perches on branches while hunting for insects to eat.

Archaeopteryx has the wings and feathers of a modern bird and is believed to have been the first bird to exist.

IS IT A BIRD?
NO, IT'S A DINOSAUR

▼ **Compsognathus** has a bird-like build and is the size of a chicken, but it is a dinosaur. It may have been covered with feathers. Feathered dinosaurs are sometimes called dino-birds.

Archaeopteryx is a primitive bird. It is thought to be the link between dinosaurs and modern-day birds.

Meaning of name: Ancient wing
Size: 50 cm (1 ft 6 in) wingspan
Family: Archaeopterygidae
Period: Late Jurassic
Weight: Up to 1 kg (2.2 lb)
Found in: Germany
Diet: Insects

▶ **Scansoriopteryx** is a feathered, sparrow-sized, tree-dwelling dinosaur. It has a very long third finger for getting insects out of tree holes.

▼ **Caudipteryx**, like other dino-birds, cannot fly. It probably wades in lakes and perches on branches.

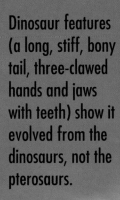

Dinosaur features (a long, stiff, bony tail, three-clawed hands and jaws with teeth) show it evolved from the dinosaurs, not the pterosaurs.

LIZARD GLIDERS

As you run through the trees after the *Archaeopteryx*, a rough wing suddenly brushes past your face, followed by the whiplash of a tail that burns your cheek. It's a *Coelurosauravus* – a gliding lizard! More creatures appear, forming a flapping mass around you. You're not feeling welcome here – it's time to get out of the forest. But you're lost, and where's the microlight?

Coelurosauravus is one of the oldest flying reptiles.

More than 20 hollow bones and skin form a web-like wing. The wings close for protection when it lands.

A long tail helps with stability as it glides and snaps up insects in the air.

OLD TIMERS

Coelurosauravus is the earliest known gliding vertebrate.

Meaning of name: Flying hollow lizard
Length: 30 cm (1 ft)
Family: Coelurosauravidae
Period: Permian
Weight: Unknown
Found in: Madagascar, Germany, England
Diet: Insects

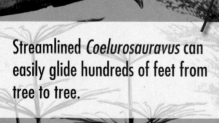

Streamlined *Coelurosauravus* can easily glide hundreds of feet from tree to tree.

▼ The earliest creatures to fly were insects, like *Meganeura* – a giant dragonfly as big as a parrot. *Meganeura* buzzed around prehistoric Carboniferous forests.

▼ Fossil evidence shows that *Meganeura*'s wingspan stretched an astonishing 75 cm (2 ft 6 in). Some scientists believe that insects were able to grow larger in the Carboniferous period because there was more oxygen in the air.

PUNK PTEROSAUR

You reach a clearing and look up into the sky. Against the bright sunlight you see the biggest pterosaur so far – the *Tapejara*. Its sharp and turned-down beak looks capable of biting off your head. The huge crest looks like a Mohican. Trembling as you film it, you wish your microlight was within sight, ready for a quick escape. You set off again, feeling more and more lost in this threatening place.

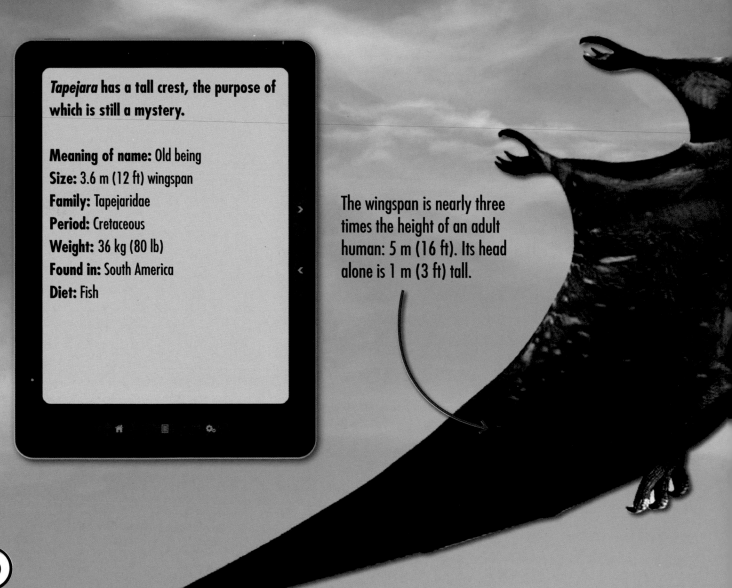

Tapejara has a tall crest, the purpose of which is still a mystery.

Meaning of name: Old being
Size: 3.6 m (12 ft) wingspan
Family: Tapejaridae
Period: Cretaceous
Weight: 36 kg (80 lb)
Found in: South America
Diet: Fish

The wingspan is nearly three times the height of an adult human: 5 m (16 ft). Its head alone is 1 m (3 ft) tall.

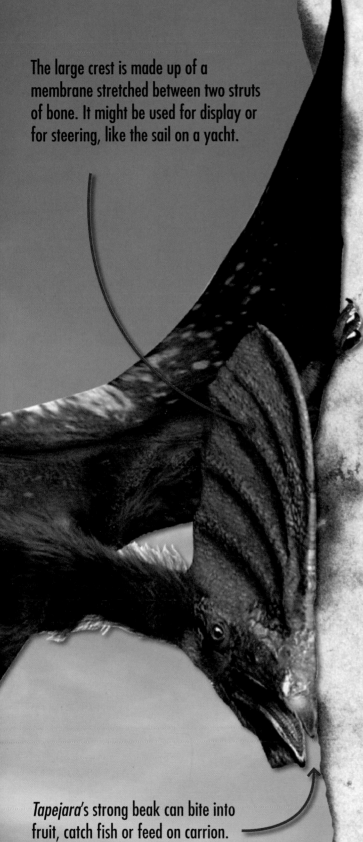

The large crest is made up of a membrane stretched between two struts of bone. It might be used for display or for steering, like the sail on a yacht.

Tapejara's strong beak can bite into fruit, catch fish or feed on carrion.

HEAD AND BEAK CRESTS

▼ Some pterosaurs, such as *Tropeognathus*, had crests on their beaks, not their heads. Crests on the lower and upper jaw perhaps helped it cut through the surface of the water as it flew low, skimming the water to catch fish.

▼ The many blood vessels in *Tupuxara's* crest may change its colour according to the creature's mood, just as anger might redden a human face.

◀ Perhaps only male pterosaurs have showy crests. Female pterosaur fossils have been found without crests, when males of the same species have them.

SEASIDE FLOCK

You reach the edge of the forest and discover not a river but a beach, crowded with a flock of noisy *Dimorphodons*. You get excellent shots of the *Dimorphodons* taking off, landing and stumbling across the rocks. Then you spot some eggs in the sand. One starts to crack... then the video screen goes blank. You've got to get back to the microlight for another battery!

The deep beak has 30 to 40 sharp pointed teeth in each jaw and is an excellent fish-catching weapon.

Perhaps *Dimorphodon*'s colourful beak is used for signalling during the breeding season.

Claws on both the feet and hands make it easy to cling to cliff faces.

The first fossil remains of *Dimorphodon* were found by Mary Anning in England in 1828.

Meaning of name: Two-formed tooth
Size: 1.3 m (4 ft) wingspan
Family: Dimorphodontidae
Period: Jurassic
Weight: 2.3 kg (5 lb)
Found in: Europe, Central America
Diet: Fish, insects, perhaps small vertebrates and carrion

CRAWLERS AND POLE-VAULTERS

Scientists used to think that *Dimorphodon* walked on two legs, but this is now seen as improbable – they were likely to fall over!

▼ It is more likely that, like other pterosaurs, *Dimophordon* leaned forward and crawled along on its two legs and two wings.

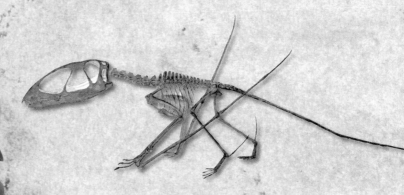

▼ For take-off, *Dimophordon* pushed off its back legs and used its wings for extra leverage – just as a pole-vaulter pushes him or herself higher with a pole.

Fish-eating birds like *Dimorphodon* may have formed nest-making colonies on cliff edges, or buried their eggs in the sand, like turtles.

THE PLUMED SERPENT

Further down the beach you find the river and follow its course back to the microlight at last. Just as you change the battery, the sky turns black. Is it a storm cloud? No, it's the most awesome thing you've seen in your life, the largest flying creature the world has known – *Quetzalcoatlus*! You jump into the microlight and join it in the sky, but you don't spot the open jaws you're heading towards…

Quetzalcoatlus flies effortlessly, hardly flapping its wings. It uses air currents to carry its weight.

Its 10–11 m (35 ft) wingspan, small body weight and shape mean it can fly up to 130 km/h (80 mph) for seven to ten days.

24

The long-necked *Quetzalcoatlus* is the largest-ever flying creature known to exist.

Meaning of name: Named after the Mesoamerican god Quetzalcoatl
Size: 9 m (30 ft) wingspan
Family: Azhdarchidae
Period: Late Cretaceous
Weight: 91 kg (200 lb)
Found in: North America
Diet: Fish and meat

Its flight range could be as far as 19,300 km (12,000 miles) — that's further than London to Sydney!

SKY-GOD

▼ *Quetzalcoatlus* is named after the sky-god Quetzalcoatl – a mythical plumed serpent, worshipped by Middle American peoples such as the Aztecs and Toltecs.

▼ Like a modern stork, *Quetzalcoatlus* may have not only eaten fish, but spent time on the ground scavenging for carrion, or eating worms and insects. It might even have preyed on small dinosaurs.

MIGRATION

Just in time, you roll the microlight and escape the toothy jaws of an *Ornithocheirus*. But then you realise you're right in the middle of a migratory flight path! Each flap of an *Ornithocheirus* wing nearly sends your craft into a spin. One gets too close – one tear to its wing and the magnificent creature will fall. Horrified, you feel like an invader in their world; you're a danger to them. It's time to fly home.

Pterosaur lungs are attached to air sacs in other parts of their bodies. Air sacs in the wings may help to keep the shape of the wings, and to maintain stability during flight.

The 'keel' shape at the end of the beak has numerous possible uses: to smash open shellfish, to frighten off rivals or to attract a mate.

Ornithocheirus is well known for the round boney crests at the tips of its upper and lower jaws.

Meaning of name: Bird hand
Size: 3–6 m (10–20 ft) wingspan
Family: Ornithocheiridae
Period: Middle Cretaceous
Weight: 23–46 kg (50–100 lb)
Found in: Western Europe, South America
Diet: Fish

Pterosaur wings are vulnerable — more so than the resilient feather covering of the first dino-birds and the birds of today.

FOSSIL PUZZLES

▼ Putting together bits of fossilised bones to make an identifiable pterosaur can be difficult, even impossible. So many fossil fragments of *Ornithocheirus* have been found that scientists have grouped them into 40 different species, without a complete skeleton of any of them!

▼ Scientist agree that pterosaurs, including *Ornithocheirus*, have been extinct for 65 million years. However, some people claim to have seen a living pterosaur around Papua New Guinea. They call it the ropen. Perhaps it is a living fossil.

FLYING MONSTER REPORT

After meeting with excited and envious paleontologists, you prepare a presentation for the public. Halls around the world sell out for your presentation, which you call 'In Search of the Plumed Serpent'. Audiences applaud when they see the best of your videos – the vast wings of *Quetzalcoatlus*.

Some of the most terrifying pterosaurs were not the biggest on your safari. Years later, your blood still runs cold when you recall the flock of tiny *Anurognathus* that fluttered around your head – and you will always bear the vampire-like scar from the one that bit your neck.

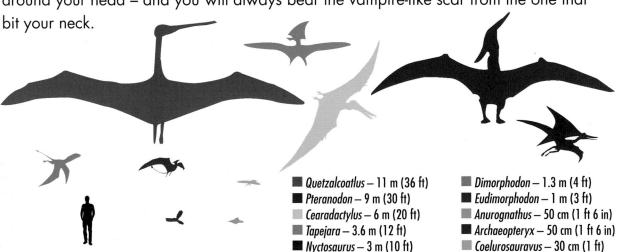

- Quetzalcoatlus – 11 m (36 ft)
- Pteranodon – 9 m (30 ft)
- Cearadactylus – 6 m (20 ft)
- Tapejara – 3.6 m (12 ft)
- Nyctosaurus – 3 m (10 ft)
- Dimorphodon – 1.3 m (4 ft)
- Eudimorphodon – 1 m (3 ft)
- Anurognathus – 50 cm (1 ft 6 in)
- Archaeopteryx – 50 cm (1 ft 6 in)
- Coelurosauravus – 30 cm (1 ft)

The creatures you saw on safari originally lived at different times throughout prehistory. This chart shows the different periods in which they lived. MYA stands for million years ago.

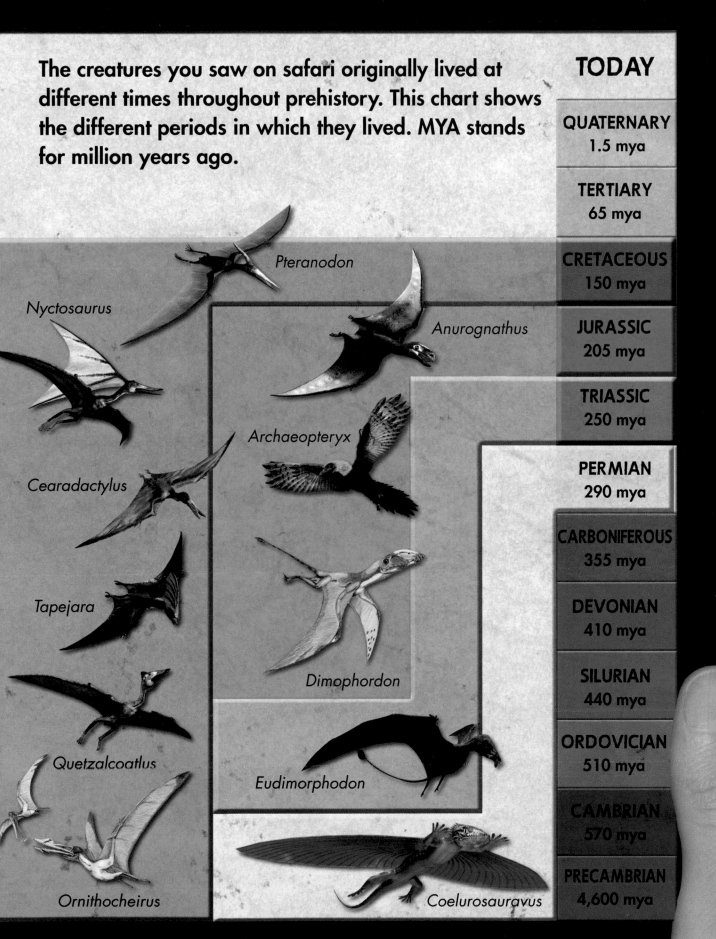

Pteranodon

Nyctosaurus

Anurognathus

Cearadactylus

Archaeopteryx

Tapejara

Dimophordon

Quetzalcoatlus

Eudimorphodon

Ornithocheirus

Coelurosauravus

TODAY	
QUATERNARY	1.5 mya
TERTIARY	65 mya
CRETACEOUS	150 mya
JURASSIC	205 mya
TRIASSIC	250 mya
PERMIAN	290 mya
CARBONIFEROUS	355 mya
DEVONIAN	410 mya
SILURIAN	440 mya
ORDOVICIAN	510 mya
CAMBRIAN	570 mya
PRECAMBRIAN	4,600 mya

GLOSSARY

air current A body of moving air, such as a breeze or a wind.

air sacs Pockets inside the lungs that are used for storing air. Some animals, such as birds, have air sacs in other parts of their bodies.

antler-like Similar to the branch-like bony growths on the heads of deer.

breeding season Months in the year when creatures gather to mate in order to have offspring.

Carboniferous A prehistoric period 355 million years ago in which there were many swamps and forests.

carrion Flesh from a creature that has died – a source of food for some birds or animals such as pterosaurs.

colonies Groups of animals living together.

crest A body part that sticks out from an animal's head.

extinct Not existing anymore; for example, dinosaurs and pterosaurs are extinct.

fangs Long sharp teeth, which are often used for biting and tearing flesh.

fibrous Made up of stringy material.

filtering Extracting food, such as tiny fish, from water by passing it through sieve-like parts of the mouth.

flamingo A pink or reddish wading bird with long legs, a long neck and a duck-like bill.

fossil Prehistoric remains such as a bone or a trace such as a footprint that has become preserved in rock.

fossilised Made into a fossil.

glider A flying creature that does not flap its wings to fly long distances, but instead swoops with outstretched wings, often from tree to tree.

keel A structure on the bottom of a boat that helps to keep it from tipping over.

living fossil A plant or creature that lives today, but also lived in prehistoric times in a similar form.

membrane A part of a creature's body that is similar to a thin skin.

microlight A tiny one- or two-seater aircraft.

oxygen A transparent gas found in the air. Animals need oxygen to live.

pole-vaulter A sportsperson who jumps over a high bar with the aid of a long pole.

prey An animal that is hunted by other animals for food.

pterosaurs Flying reptiles that were closely related to the dinosaurs.

reptiles Animals that have scales and lay eggs, such as snakes and tortoises. Modern reptiles are cold-blooded; however, some prehistoric reptiles were warm-blooded.

rudder A part of an aircraft that keeps it upright and helps to steer it.

solar panel A panel that absorbs sunlight and turns it into warmth or electricity.

spoonbill A tall wading bird that has a long bill with a flat tip.

stability Steadiness.

stork A tall wading bird with a long, heavy bill. The stork is often white and black in colour.

Triassic A prehistoric period 250 million years ago when many creatures became extinct and others, such as pterosaurs, gradually took their place.

warm-blooded Able to maintain body heat without needing to bask in the sun to get warm.

wingspan The measurement from one wingtip to the other, when the wings are outstretched.

FURTHER READING

Archaeopteryx: The First Bird (Graphic Dinosaurs) by Rob Shone (PowerKids Press, 2007)

DK Eyewitness: Fossil by Paul Taylor (Dorling Kindersley, 2004)

The Mystery of the Death of the Dinosaurs (Can Science Solve?) by Chris Oxlade (Heinemann Library, 2008)

Naturetrails: Rocks and Fossils (Usborne Nature Trail) by Struan Reid (Usborne Publishing, 2010)

Prehistoric Life (Eyewitness Project Books) (Dorling Kindersley, 2009)

Prehistoric World (Just the Facts) by Dougal Dixon (TickTock Books, 2006)

Pteranodon: The Giant of the Sky (Graphic Dinosaurs) by David West (PowerKids Press, 2007)

WEBSITES

http://www.bbc.co.uk/news/science-environment-11756858 Pterosaur – Watch a pterosaur pole-vault

*http://www.enchantedlearning.com/subjects/dinosaurs/glossary/indexme.shtml Dinosaur and Paleontology Dictionary: an A–Z of terms

www.historyforkids.org/scienceforkids/geology/eras/ Geological eras – discover what animals and plants lived through prehistory

http://www.jurassiccoast.com Kids' Zone – Watch a video: How do fossils form?

http://science.nationalgeographic.com/science/prehistoric-world/prehistoric-time-line/ A Prehistoric Timeline

INDEX